Wonders and Signs
The Miracles of Jesus

by John Paul II

Introduction by
Fr. Benedict J. Groeschel, CFR, Ed. D.

St. Paul Books & Media

Library of Congress Cataloging-in-Publication Data

John Paul II, Pope, 1920-
    Wonders and signs : the miracles of Jesus / by John Paul II ;
introduction by Benedict J. Groeschel.
      p.   cm.
    Talks given at the general audiences, Nov. 11, 1987–Jan. 13, 1988.
    Reprinted from L'Osservatore romano, English edition.
    Includes index.
    ISBN 0-8198-8238-0
    1. Jesus Christ—Miracles—Papal documents.   I. Title.
BT366.J64   1990   89-30953
232.9'55—dc19   CIP

Reprinted with permission from *L'Osservatore Romano*, English Edition.

Copyright © 1990 by the Daughters of St. Paul

Printed and published in the U.S.A. by St. Paul Books & Media
50 St. Paul's Ave., Boston, MA 02130

St. Paul Books & Media is the publishing house of the Daughters of St. Paul, an international congregation of women religious serving the Church with the communications media.

1 2 3 4 5 6 7 8 9   98 97 96 95 94 93 92 91 90

Contents

Introduction 7

Christ's Miracles: Fact and Significance
General Audience: November 11, 1987 11

"I Say to You, Arise!"
General Audience: November 18, 1987 19

Miraculous Signs Reveal Christ's Power
General Audience: November 25, 1987 27

Salvific "Signs"
General Audience: December 2, 1987 37

Christ's Miracles:
   Manifestations of Salvific Love
General Audience: December 9, 1987 45

Miracles: A Call to Faith
General Audience: December 16, 1987 53

Christ's Miracles:
   Manifestations of the Supernatural Order
General Audience: January 13, 1988 61

Index 69

Introduction

This series of talks given by Pope John Paul II at the general audiences from November 11, 1987 to January 13, 1988, on the miracles of Christ are extremely important for anyone interested in Christian education or apologetics. The Holy Father not only relates the miracles and signs performed by Christ to his mission and to his claim to be the only begotten Son of God sent into the world by the love of the Father, but he also reaffirms their historical reality. All too often Christians are treated to symbolic interpretations of the miracles and signs done by Christ and these theories are presented as fact or even the doctrine of the Church.

St. Peter in the first catechetical instruction spoke of Jesus of Nazareth as "a man attested to by God with mighty works and wonders and signs" (Acts 2:22). Along with many scholars, the Holy Father sees an intrinsic and necessary connection between Christ's ability to work miracles of nature, of physical and psychological healing, and his claim to be the Messiah. As the distinguished Scripture scholar Rudolph Schnackenberg extensively demonstrates, Jesus used his miraculous powers to call human beings to faith in his proclamation of the kingdom, his messiahship, and even his divinity (*The Moral Teaching of the New Testament,* London; Burns & Oates, 1964).

The Holy Father does not hesitate to identify the intellectual bias against accepting the historical reality of the miracles of Christ as a "rationalistic prejudice" against the supernatural. The argument usually maintains that our modern scientific view of the world has done away with the miraculous, that is, the suspension of the laws of nature by divine power. This prejudice ignores two very important intellectual issues. The first is that it is not the province of science as presently defined to either accept or reject miracles. It is possible, however, for natural science to identify "cures" which are empirically demonstrated, instantaneous, complete, and without any scientific explanation. The anti-supernatural prejudice of certain Scripture scholars fails to take into account that such curative events occur in our own day and are certified by scientists with impeccable credentials. Such cures have been certified in recent years by the Medical Bureau of Lourdes as well as the ad hoc medical committees of the Congregation for the Beatification and Canonization of Saints. It is difficult to see how a Christian writer can dismiss the historical reality of the miracles of Christ on the a priori argument that science has proved miraculous cures to be impossible, when, in fact, as the Holy Father asserts, they happen in our own day (cf. January 13, 1988).

If, in the scientific community it is considered dishonest to ignore evidence pertinent to a particular question under study, the same rule should apply when the claim is made that scientific principles are being used in the study of Sacred Scripture. An intellectually unwarranted minimalism can deprive Christians of the immense spiritual riches to be gained from the understanding of the relationship of Christ's miracles to his mission as Savior and Redeemer. The historical reality of the miracles, including the supreme miracle of the resurrection, is a necessary foundation for appreciating the even more profound effects of the Incarnation and the Redemption. The Holy Father quotes St. Augustine: "The miracles worked by our Lord, Jesus Christ, are divine works which raise the human mind above visible things to understand what is divine" (Io. Ev. Tr., 24, 1).

If the miracles of Christ are reduced to myths or literary devices used to communicate truths to simple minds, the very profound spiritual realities which these miracles anticipate and verify can be called into doubt. This is exactly what happens. As the Holy Father demonstrates, it is far more intellectually honest and consistent with Revelation to see these miracles and signs as historical realities which actually occurred in the time of our Lord and which, ever since, point to the transcendent realities of salvation. He again quotes St. Augustine in a powerful text (November 25, 1987): "If we consider now the deeds worked by our Lord and Savior, Jesus Christ, we see that the eyes of the blind, miraculously opened, were closed by death, and the limbs of the paralyzed, miraculously restored, were again immobilized in death. All that was temporarily cured in the mortal body was in the end undone; but the soul that believed passed to eternal life. With this infirm man the Lord wished to give a great sign to the soul that would have believed, for the remission of whose sins he had come, and whose weaknesses he had healed by the humiliation of himself" (Augustine, In Io. Ev. Tr., 17, 1).

A prayerful and energetic study of this brief collection will reward the reader with much material for meditation, and with authoritative arguments for correcting popular prejudice against the supernatural in the study of the Gospels. Most of all it will provide an antidote to unwarranted minimalism which causes the life and message of our Lord, Jesus Christ, to become more and more obscure. For those who are growing in faith, this figure of Jesus does not become more obscure but by devout study of the scriptures and tradition becomes more luminous and bright.

Fr. Benedict J. Groeschel, CFR., Ed. D.

Christ's Miracles:
Fact and Significance

On the day of Pentecost, after receiving the light and power of the Holy Spirit, Peter bore clear and courageous witness to Christ crucified and risen. "Men of Israel," he proclaimed, "hear these words: Jesus of Nazareth, a man attested to you by God with mighty works and wonders and signs...you crucified...and killed. But God raised him up, releasing him from the pangs of death" (cf. Acts 2:22-24).

This testimony includes a synthesis of the whole messianic activity of Jesus of Nazareth, whom God had commended by "mighty deeds, wonders and signs." It also constitutes an outline of the first Christian catechesis, offered to us by the very head of the apostolic college, Peter.

After nearly two thousand years the present successor of Peter, in developing his reflections on Jesus Christ, must now deal with the content of that first apostolic catechesis on the very day of Pentecost. Until now we have spoken of the Son of man who by his teaching made it known that he was the true Son of God, that he and the Father "are one" (cf. Jn 10:30). His word was accompanied by "mighty works, wonders and signs." These deeds accompanied the words, not only following them by way of confirming their authenticity, but frequently preceding them, as the Acts of the Apostles give us to understand when speaking "of all that Jesus did and taught from the beginning" (cf. Acts 1:1). It was those same words and particularly "the marvels and signs" which testified that "the kingdom of God was at hand" (cf. Mk 1:15), that with Jesus it had entered into the earthly history of mankind and was eager to enter into every human spirit. At the same time they were a witness that he who performed them was truly the Son of God. For this reason it is necessary to link these present reflections on Christ's mighty deeds and signs with the previous ones on his divine sonship.

Before proceeding step by step in analyzing the significance of these "wonders and signs" (as Peter had very specifically defined them on the day of Pentecost), one must note that they (the wonders and signs) certainly pertain to the integral content of the Gospels as eyewitness testimonies to Christ. It is not in fact possible to exclude the mighty deeds from the gospel text and context. The analysis of not only the text but also of the context speaks in favor of their "historical" character; it attests that they are facts which actually happened, and that they were really performed by Christ. Whoever approaches the matter with intellectual honesty and scientific expertise cannot dispose of them in a few words as simply later inventions.

In this regard it is well to observe that these facts are not only attested to and narrated by the apostles and disciples of Jesus, but in many cases they are admitted by his opponents. For example, it is very significant that they did not deny the reality of the miracles performed by Jesus, but that they attributed them to the power of Satan. For they said: "He is possessed by Beelzebul," and "by the prince of demons he drives out demons" (cf. Mk 3:22; also Mt 12:24; Lk 11:14-15). Jesus, however, clearly pointed out the contradiction in these remarks. He said: "If Satan has risen up against himself and is divided, he cannot stand, but is coming to an end" (cf. Mk 3:26). The most important thing for us at the moment, then, is the fact that even Jesus' opponents could not deny his "mighty deeds, wonders and signs" as reality—as facts which had actually taken place.

It is also a notable fact that Jesus' opponents watched him to see whether he would heal on the sabbath, and thus they would be in a position to accuse him of transgressing the Old Testament Law. This was stated in the case of the man with the withered hand (cf. Mk 3:1-2).

To be considered also is Jesus' reply, not to his opponents, but this time to the messengers sent by John the Baptist to ask him: "Are you the one who is to come, or should we look for another?" (cf. Mt 11:3) Jesus replies: "Go and tell John what you hear and see: the blind regain their sight, the lame walk, lepers are cleansed, the deaf hear, the dead are raised, and the poor have the good news proclaimed to them" (cf. Mt 11:4-5; also Lk 7:22). Jesus' reply refers to Isaiah's prophecy about the future Messiah (cf. Is

35:5-6), which could undoubtedly be understood in the sense of a renewal of a spiritual healing of Israel and of humanity. But in the gospel context, from the mouth of Jesus, it indicates facts commonly known and which the Baptist's disciples can report to him as signs of Christ's messiahship.

All the evangelists record the facts to which Peter refers on the day of Pentecost: "mighty deeds, wonders and signs" (cf. Acts 2:22). The synoptics narrate many individual events, but at times they also use generalized expressions. Thus, for example, in Mark's Gospel: "He cured many who were sick with various diseases, and he drove out many demons" (cf. 1:34). Likewise Matthew and Luke: "...curing every disease and illness among the people" (cf. Mt 4:23); "...power came forth from him and healed them all" (cf. Lk 6:19). They are expressions which give us to understand the great number of miracles performed by Jesus. In John's Gospel we do not find such expressions, but rather the detailed description of seven events which the Evangelist calls "signs" (and not miracles). He thereby wishes to indicate the most essential element of those facts, namely, the revelation of God's action in Jesus, while the word "miracle" indicates rather the "extraordinary" aspect of those events in the eyes of those who saw or who heard them spoken of. Before concluding his Gospel, John however also considers it important to mention that "Jesus did many other signs in the presence of his disciples that are not written in this book" (cf. Jn 20:30). He then gives the reason for the choices he has made:

"These are written that you may believe that Jesus is the Messiah, the Son of God, and that through this belief you may have life in his name" (cf. Jn 20:31). This is the aim of both the synoptics and the fourth Gospel: to show by means of the miracles the truth of the Son of God and to lead to the faith which is the beginning of salvation.

Anyway, when the Apostle Peter, on the day of Pentecost, bears witness to the entire mission of Jesus of Nazareth, attested to by God with "mighty deeds, wonders and signs," he cannot but recall that the same Jesus was crucified and risen (cf. Acts 2:22-24). He thus indicates the paschal event in which is offered the most complete sign of God's saving and redemptive action in the history of humanity. In this sign is enclosed, one might say, the "anti-miracle" of the death on the cross and the "miracle" of the resurrection (miracle of miracles) which are rooted in a single mystery, so that in it the human person can read to the very depths of God's self-revelation in Jesus Christ, and by adhering to it by faith enter upon the way of salvation.

"I Say to You, Arise!"

If we examine attentively the "mighty works and wonders and signs" spoken of by the Apostle Peter on Pentecost day in Jerusalem and provided by God as a proof of the credibility of Jesus Christ's mission, we note that Jesus, in performing these "miraculous signs," acted in his own name. He was conscious of his own name, conscious of his divine power and at the same time conscious of his intimate union with the Father. Once again and always we are in the presence of the mystery of the "Son of man—Son of God," whose identity transcends all limits of the human condition (although belonging to it by his own free choice), and all possibility of human achievement and even of knowledge.

A glance at some individual events recorded by the evangelists enables us to take note of that mysterious presence in whose name Jesus Christ performs his miracles. For example, in response to the entreaties of the leper who begs him: "If you will, you can cure me!" Jesus, in his human nature, "moved with compassion," gives a word of command which, in such a case, is proper to God and not to a mere human being: "I do will it. Be made clean!" The leprosy left him immediately, and he was made clean (cf. Mk 1:40-42). Similarly in the case of the paralytic who was let through an opening made in the roof of the house: "I say to you, rise. Pick up your mat, and go home" (cf. Mk 2:1-12).

Again, in the case of Jairus' daughter we read that "he [Jesus] took the child by the hand, and said to her, 'Talitha koum' which means, 'Little girl, I say to you, arise!' The dead girl sat up and began to speak" (cf. Mk 5:41-42).

In so many of these episodes we see, apparent from Jesus' words, the expression of a will and a power to which he interiorly appeals and which he expresses, one might say, with the greatest naturalness—as though the power to give people health, healing and even to bring the dead back to life, belonged to his own mysterious condition.

Of particular note is the raising of Lazarus described in detail by St. John. We read: "Jesus looked upward and said: 'Father, I thank you for having heard me. I know that you always hear me, but I have said this for the sake of the crowd, that they may believe that you sent me.' Having said this, he called loudly, 'Lazarus, come out!' And the dead man came out" (cf. Jn 11:41-44). In the precise description of this event it is emphasized that Jesus raised his friend Lazarus from the dead by his own power and in close union with the Father. Here we find clear confirmation of Jesus' words: "My Father is working still and I am working" (cf. Jn 5:17). Moreover, it could be said that we have here an anticipated demonstration of what Jesus will say in the Upper Room during his Last Supper conversation with the apostles concerning his relations with the Father, and, indeed, concerning his identity in being with the Father.

The Gospels show by various miracles-signs that the divine power at work in Jesus Christ extends beyond the human world and is revealed as a power of dominion also over the forces of nature. The calming of the tempest is significant: "Meanwhile a great storm of wind arose." The terrified fishermen-apostles wakened Jesus, who had been asleep in the stern. He "woke-up, rebuked the wind, and said to the sea, 'Quiet! Be still!' The wind ceased and there was great calm...[the apostles] were filled with great awe and said to one another, 'Who then is this whom even wind and sea obey?'" (cf. Mk 4:37-41)

This series of events included the miraculous catches of fish which took place at Jesus' command *(in verbo tuo)* after previous attempts had failed (cf. Lk 5:4-6; Jn 21:3-6). The same can also be said, as regards the structure of the event, of the "first sign" performed at Cana in Galilee, when Jesus ordered the servants to fill the jars with water and then to bring "the water changed into wine" to the headwaiter (cf. Jn 2:7-9). As in the miraculous catches of fish, so likewise at Cana in Galilee, people play their part: the fishermen-apostles in one case, and the servants at the marriage feast in the other. It is clear, however, that the extraordinary effect of the action does not come from them, but from him who had given them the order to act, and who works with his mysterious divine power.

This is confirmed by the reaction of the apostles, and especially of Peter who, after the miraculous catch of fish, "fell at the knees of Jesus and said, 'Depart from me, Lord, for I am a sinful man'" (cf. Lk 5:8). It is one of the many cases of emotional feeling which assumes the form of reverential awe or even of fear, both in the apostles as in the case of Simon Peter, and also in the people when they feel touched by the wing of the divine mystery.

On a day after the ascension, those who will witness "the wonders and signs...done through the apostles" (cf. Acts 2:43) will be seized by a similar "awe." According to Acts, the people "carried the sick out into the streets and laid them on cots and mats so that when Peter came by, at least his shadow might fall on one or another of them" (cf. Acts 5:15). However, these "wonders and signs" which accompanied the beginnings of the apostolic Church were done by the apostles, not in their own name, but in the name of Jesus Christ, and were therefore a further proof of his divine power. One is impressed by Peter's reply and command to the crippled man who had asked him for an alms near the gate of the Temple of Jerusalem: "'I have neither silver nor gold, but what I do have I give you: in the name of Jesus Christ of Nazareth, walk.' And he took him by the right hand and raised him up; and immediately his feet and ankles were made strong" (cf. Acts 3:6-7). One recalls also what Peter said to the paralyzed man named Aeneas: "'Jesus Christ heals you. Get up and make your bed.' And he got up at once" (cf. Acts 9:34).

Also the other prince of the apostles, Paul, when recalling in the Letter to the Romans all that he had done as "minister of Christ among the pagans," hastens to add that his sole merit is to be found in that ministry: "For I will not dare to speak of anything except what Christ has accomplished through me to lead the Gentiles to obedience by word and deed, by the power of signs and wonders, by the power of the Spirit" (cf. Rom 15:18-19).

In the early period of the Church and especially in the evangelization of the world carried out by the apostles, those "mighty works, wonders and signs" abounded, as Jesus himself had promised them (cf. Acts 2:22). But it can be said that they have always been repeated throughout salvation history, especially in decisive moments in order to put into effect God's plan. Thus it was in the Old Testament in regard to the "Exodus" of Israel from the bondage of Egypt and the journey to the Promised Land under the leadership of Moses. When with the incarnation of the Son of God "the fullness of time had come" (cf. Gal 4:4), those miraculous signs of the divine action take on a new value and a new efficacy through the divine authority of Christ and through reference to his Name—and therefore to his truth, promise, command and glory—with which they are performed by the apostles and by so many saints in the Church. Miracles happen even today, and in each of them is outlined the face of the "Son of man—Son of God," and an affirmation of a gift of grace and salvation.

Miraculous Signs Reveal Christ's Power

A text from St. Augustine offers us the key for interpreting Christ's miracles as signs of his saving power: "The fact that he became man for us contributed more to our salvation than the miracles he performed among us. His healing of the evils of the soul is more important than the curing of the illnesses of the body which is doomed to death" (Augustine, In Io. Ev. Tr. 17, 1). For the salvation of the soul and the redemption of the whole world Jesus performed miracles of the corporeal order also. By means of the "mighty deeds, wonders and signs" which he performed, Jesus Christ manifested his power to save mankind from the evil which threatens the immortal soul and the call to union with God.

This is revealed particularly in the healing of the paralytic of Capernaum. Since those who carried him were unable to enter by the door into the house where Jesus was teaching, they lowered the sick man through an opening in the roof so that he found himself at the feet of the Master. "Jesus, on seeing their faith, said to the paralytic, 'Child, your sins are forgiven.'" These words aroused among some of those present the suspicion of blasphemy: "This man is blaspheming!

Who but God can forgive sins?" As though in response to those who had entertained these thoughts, Jesus said to those present: "Which is easier, to say to the paralytic, 'Your sins are forgiven,' or to say, 'Rise, pick up your mat and walk'? But that you may know that the Son of man has authority to forgive sins on earth"—he said to the paralytic—"'I say to you, rise, pick up your mat, and go home.' He rose, picked up his mat at once, and went away in the sight of everyone" (cf. Mk 2:1-12; Mt 9:1-8; Lk 5:18-26; "...he went home glorifying God" Lk 5:25).

Jesus himself explains in this case that the miracle of curing the paralytic is a sign of the saving power whereby he forgives sins. Jesus performs this sign to show that he had come as Savior of the world whose principal task was to free mankind from spiritual evil—the evil that separates man from God and impedes salvation in God. And that evil is sin.

With the same key one can explain that special category of Christ's miracles, "the driving out of demons." "Unclean spirit, come out of the man!" Jesus orders according to Mark's Gospel when he met the man in the territory of the Gerasenes, who had an unclean spirit (cf. Mk 5:8). On the occasion we witness an unusual conversation. When that "unclean spirit" feels threatened by Christ, he cries out against him: "What have you to do with me, Jesus, Son of the Most High God? I adjure you by God do not torment me!" Jesus asked him, "What is your name?" He replies, "Legion is my name. There are many of us" (cf. Mk 5:7-9). We are therefore on the margin of an obscure world involving physical and psychical factors. Factors which undoubtedly play their part in causing pathological conditions in which is inserted that demonic reality, variously represented and described in human language, but radically hostile to God and therefore to man and to Christ who had come to free humanity from the power of evil. But even the "unclean spirit," in spite of himself, in that clash with the other presence, bursts out into that admission coming from a perverse but lucid intelligence: "Son of the Most High God."

In Mark's Gospel we find also the description of the event usually described as the cure of the epileptic. In fact the symptoms narrated by the evangelist are characteristic also of this disease (foaming at the mouth, grinding of teeth, and bodily rigidity). However, the father of the epileptic presents his son to Jesus, describing him as one possessed by an evil spirit, who throws him into fits of convulsions, casts him down on the ground, and the unfortunate youth rolls about foaming at the mouth. It is indeed possible that in such a state of illness the evil one might insinuate himself in and play a part. But even admitting that it was a case of epilepsy from which Jesus cures the youth repudiated by his father as possessed by a devil, it is, however, significant that Jesus effects the cure by ordering the "mute and deaf spirit": "Come out of him and never enter him again" (cf. Mk 9:17-27). It is a reaffirmation of his mission and of his power to free the human person radically from spiritual evil.

Jesus makes his mission clearly known: to free humanity from evil and first of all from sin—spiritual evil. It is a mission which implies and explains his struggle with the evil spirit who is the prime author of evil in the history of mankind. As we read in the Gospels, Jesus repeatedly declares that this is the meaning of his work and that of his apostles. Thus in Luke: "I have observed Satan fall like lightning from the sky. Behold, I have given you the power to tread...upon the full force of the enemy and nothing will harm you" (cf. Lk 10:18-19). According to Mark, Jesus after having appointed the Twelve, sent them forth "to preach and to have authority to drive out demons" (cf. Mk 3:14-15). According to Luke also, the seventy-two disciples, after returning from their first mission, report to Jesus: "Lord, even the demons are subject to us because of your name" (cf. Lk 10:17).

Thus is manifested the power of the Son of man over sin and over the author of sin. The name of Jesus, by virtue of which even the demons are subject, means Savior. However, this saving power of his will has its definitive fulfillment in the sacrifice of the cross. The cross will mark the complete victory over Satan and sin because this is the Father's plan which his only-begotten Son fulfills by becoming man—to conquer in weakness, and to attain the glory of the resurrection and of life by means of the humiliation of the cross. Even in this paradox there shines forth the divine power which can rightly be called the "power of the cross."

Even the victory over death, the dramatic consequence of sin, forms part of this power and belongs to the mission of the Savior of the world manifested by "mighty deeds, wonders and signs." The victory over sin and over death marks the way of the messianic mission of Jesus from Nazareth to Calvary. Among the "signs" which particularly mark his journey toward the victory over death there are especially the cases of people raised from the dead. "The dead are raised" (cf. Mt 11:5) was, in fact, the answer given by Jesus to the messengers of John the Baptist (cf. Mt 11:3) when they questioned him whether he was the Messiah. Among the various dead people raised to life by Jesus, the case of Lazarus of Bethany merits special attention. His resurrection is, as it were, a "prelude" to the cross and resurrection of Christ by which is achieved the definitive victory over sin and death.

The Evangelist John has left us a detailed description of this event. Let it suffice for us to refer to the final moment. Jesus asks that the stone which closes the tomb be removed ("Take away the stone"). Martha, the dead man's sister, observes that her brother has been dead for four days and that by now there will be a stench. Nevertheless Jesus cries out with a loud voice, "'Lazarus, come out!' And the dead man came out," the Evangelist tells us (cf. Jn 11:38-43). This fact causes many of those present to believe in him. Others, however, go to the representatives of the Sanhedrin to report the event. The chief priests and the pharisees are alarmed, thinking of the possible reaction of the Roman occupying power ("the Romans will come and take away both our land and our nation," cf. Jn 11:45-48). At that very moment Caiphas' famous words broke the silence of the Sanhedrin: "You know nothing, nor do you consider that it is better for you that one man should die instead of the people, so that the whole nation may not perish." The Evangelist notes: "He did not say this on his own, but since he was high priest for that year, he prophesied." What was the nature of the prophecy? John gives us the Christian understanding of those words: "Jesus was to die for the nation, and not only for the nation, but also to gather into one the dispersed children of God" (cf. Jn 11:49-52).

As is evident, John's description of the resurrection of Lazarus contains also the essential indications regarding the salvific significance of this miracle. They are definitive indications, because it was then that the Sanhedrin decided to put Jesus to death (cf. Jn 11:53). It will be the redemptive death "for the nation" and "to gather into one the dispersed children of God," for the salvation of the world. But Jesus has already said that that death will become the definitive victory over death. On the occasion of the resurrection of Lazarus he assured Martha: "I am the resurrection and the life; whoever believes in me, even if he dies, shall live, and everyone who lives and believes in me shall never die" (cf. Jn 11:25-26).

We turn once more to the text of St. Augustine: "If we consider now the deeds worked by our Lord and Savior, Jesus Christ, we see that the eyes of the blind, miraculously opened, were closed by death, and the limbs of the paralyzed, miraculously restored, were again immobilized in death. All that was temporarily cured in the mortal body, was in the end undone; but the soul that believed passed to eternal life. With this infirm man the Lord wished to give a great sign to the soul that would have believed, for the remission of whose sins he had come, and whose weaknesses he had healed by the humiliation of himself" (Augustine, In Io. Ev. Tr., 17, 1).

Yes, all the "mighty deeds, wonders and signs" of Christ are for the purpose of revealing him as Messiah, as Son of God; for the revelation of him who alone has the power to free mankind from sin and from death, of him who is truly the Savior of the world.

Salvific "Signs"

There is no doubt about the fact that in the Gospels Christ's miracles are presented as signs of the kingdom of God which has entered the history of mankind and the history of the world. "If I drive out demons by the Spirit of God, then the kingdom of God has come upon you," says Jesus (cf. Mt 12:28). Whatever may be said or has been said on the subject of miracles, it is certain that one cannot separate from the authentic gospel context, the "mighty deeds, wonders and signs" attributed to Jesus and even to his apostles and disciples "working in his name." In the apostolic preaching from which the Gospels principally derive, the early Christians heard the testimony of eyewitnesses about those extraordinary events which had occurred in the recent past and could therefore be checked under the critical-historical aspect. For that reason they were not surprised that they were included in the Gospels. Regardless of the objections in later times, one thing emerges as certain from the genuine sources of Christ's life and teaching. The apostles, the evangelists, and the whole primitive Church saw in each of those miracles the supreme power of Christ over nature and its laws. He who reveals God as Father, Creator and Lord of creation when performing miracles by his own power, reveals himself as Son, one in being with the Father and equal to him in lordship over creation.

Some miracles, however, present other aspects which complement the basic significance of proof of the divine power of the Son of man in the order of the economy of salvation.

Speaking thus of the first "sign" performed at Cana in Galilee, the Evangelist John observes that by means of that sign "Jesus manifested his glory and his disciples believed in him" (cf. Jn 2:11). The miracle therefore had a finality of faith, but it takes place during a wedding feast. One may therefore say that—at least in the Evangelist's intention—the "sign" serves to emphasize the whole divine economy of the covenant and of grace which is frequently expressed in the image of marriage in the books of the Old and New Testaments. The miracle at Cana of Galilee could therefore be related to the parable of the wedding feast which a king had prepared for his son, and with the eschatological "kingdom of heaven" which "is similar" to such a banquet (cf. Mt 22:2). Jesus' first miracle could be understood as a "sign" of this kingdom especially since "Jesus' hour," the hour of his passion and glorification, had not yet arrived (cf. Jn 2:4; 7:30; 8:20; 12:23-27; 13:1; 17:1). That "hour" was to be prepared by the preaching of the "gospel of the kingdom" (cf. Jn 4:23; Mt 9:35), and the miracle obtained through Mary's intercession can be considered as a "sign" and a symbolic announcement of what was about to happen.

The miracle of the multiplication of the loaves which took place near Capernaum can be understood much more clearly as a "sign" of the economy of salvation. John links it to the discourse given by Jesus the following day in which he insists on the necessity of acquiring "the food that does not perish" through "faith in him who has sent me" (cf. Jn 6:29). And Jesus speaks of himself as the true bread which "gives life to the world" (cf. Jn 6:33) and indeed as the one who gives his flesh "for the life of the world" (cf. Jn 6:51). The preannouncement of the salvific passion and death is clear, and not without reference to, and preparation for the Eucharist which was to be instituted on the day before his passion as the sacrament-bread of eternal life (cf. Jn 6:52-58).

The calming of the storm on the Lake of Genesareth can be understood as a "sign" of the constant presence of Christ in the "barque" of the Church frequently exposed to the fury of winds during periods of storm in the course of history. Jesus, wakened by the disciples, rebuked the wind and the sea and there was a great calm. Then he said to them: "Why are you terrified? Do you not yet have faith?" (cf. Mk 4:39) In this, as in other events, one perceives Jesus' will to inculcate in the apostles and disciples faith in his operative and protective presence even during the most tempestuous periods of history when the human spirit might be tempted to doubt Jesus' divine assistance. In fact, Christian preaching and spirituality frequently interpret the miracle as a "sign" of Jesus' presence and a guarantee of trust in him on the part of Christians and of the Church.

Jesus, who goes toward his disciples walking on the water, offers them another "sign" of his presence and gives an assurance of a constant watchfulness over his disciples and the Church. "Take courage, it is I, do not be afraid!" Jesus says to the apostles who had thought he was a ghost (cf. Mk 6:49-50; Mt 14:26a-27; Jn 6:16-21). Mark notes the apostles' astonishment "because they had not understood the incident of the loaves and their hearts were hardened" (cf. Mk 6:52). Matthew recounts Peter's question and his desire to get out of the boat and walk on the water toward Jesus. He records Peter's fear and his cry for help when he saw that he was about to sink. Jesus saves him but gently rebukes him: "Oh, you of little faith, why did you doubt?" (cf. Mt 14:31) Matthew also adds that "those who were in the boat did him homage, saying, 'Truly, you are the Son of God'" (cf. Mt 14:33).

The miraculous catches of fish are, for the apostles and the Church, the "signs" of the fruitfulness of their mission if they remain deeply united to Christ's saving power (cf. Lk 5:4-10; Jn 21:3-6). Indeed, Luke includes in the narrative the fact that Peter threw himself at the knees of Jesus exclaiming: "Depart from me, Lord, for I am a sinful man" (cf. Lk 5:8). Jesus replied: "Do not be afraid; from now on you will be catching men" (cf. Lk 5:10). John in his turn follows up the catch of fish after the resurrection with

Christ's command to Peter: "Feed my lambs, feed my sheep" (cf. Jn 21:15-17). It is a very significant association.

It can be said, therefore, that Christ's miracles—a manifestation of the divine omnipotence in regard to creation, revealed in his messianic power over people and things—are at the same time, the "signs" which reveal the divine work of salvation. This is the economy of salvation which is introduced with Christ, is realized definitively in the history of the human race, and is thus inscribed in this visible world which is also a divine work. The people—like the apostles on the lake—seeing Christ's miracles ask themselves: "Who is this whom even wind and sea obey?" (cf. Mk 4:41) Through these signs they are prepared to welcome the salvation offered to humanity by God in his Son.

This is the essential scope of all the miracles and signs wrought by Christ in the presence of his contemporaries, and of those miracles which—in the course of history—will be performed by his apostles and disciples in reference to the saving power of his Name: "In the name of Jesus Christ of Nazareth, walk!" (cf. Acts 3:16)

Christ's Miracles: Manifestations of Salvific Love

Christ's miracles, recorded in the Gospels, are "signs" of the divine omnipotence and of the salvific power of the Son of man, and also the revelation of God's love for humanity—particularly for those who suffer, who are in need, who implore healing, pardon and compassion. They are therefore "signs" of the merciful love proclaimed in the Old and New Testaments (cf. Encyclical *Dives in Misericordia*). Especially the reading of the Gospel makes us understand and almost "feel" that Jesus' miracles have their source in God's loving and merciful heart which lives and beats in Jesus' human heart. Jesus performs miracles to overcome every kind of evil existing in the world: physical evil, moral evil which is sin, and finally him who is "the father of sin" in the history of humanity, namely, Satan.

The miracles are therefore "for man." They are works of Jesus which, in harmony with the redemptive finality of his mission, re-establish the good where evil lurks producing disorder and confusion. Those who accept them, who are present at them, are aware of this fact, so much so that, according to Mark, "they were exceedingly astonished and said, 'He has done all things well. He makes the deaf hear and the mute speak'" (cf. Mk 7:37).

An attentive study of the gospel texts reveals that no motive other than love for humanity—merciful love—explains the "mighty deeds and signs" of the Son of man. In the Old Testament Elijah made use of "fire from heaven" to confirm his power as a prophet and to punish incredulity (cf. 2 Kings 1:10). When the Apostles James and John sought to persuade Jesus to punish with "fire from heaven" a Samaritan village which had refused them hospitality, he definitely forbade them to make such a request. The Evangelist mentions categorically that "he turned and rebuked them" (cf. Lk 9:55). (Many codices including the Vulgate add: "You do not know what manner of spirit you are; for the Son of man came not to destroy men's lives but to save them.") Jesus never worked a miracle to punish anyone, not even the guilty.

In this regard the detail connected with Jesus' arrest in the garden of Gethsemane is significant. Peter was ready to defend his Master with the sword, and he even "struck the high priest's servant and cut off his right ear. The servant's name was Malchus" (cf. Jn 18:10). But Jesus forbade him to use the sword. Indeed, "he touched the servant's ear and healed him" (cf. Lk 22:51). It is further proof that Jesus does not perform miracles for his own defense. He tells his followers that he could call upon his Father for "more than twelve legions of angels" (cf. Mt 26:53) to save him from the enemies who surround him. All that he does, even in working miracles, is done in close union with the Father. He does it for the sake of the kingdom of God, and of the salvation of mankind. He does it for love.

Thus, at the beginning of his Messianic mission, Jesus rejected the devil's suggestions to perform "mighty works," for example, to change stones into loaves of bread (cf. Mt 4:3-4). The power of the Messiah was granted to him not for pretentious display or vainglory. He who came "to bear witness to the truth" (cf. Jn 18:37), who indeed is "the truth" (cf. Jn 14:6) always works in absolute conformity with his salvific mission. All his "wonders and signs" express this conformity in the framework of the "Messianic mystery" of God which is, as it were, concealed in the nature of the Son of man, as is shown by the Gospels, especially that of Mark. If in the miracles there is almost always a radiance of the divine power which the disciples and people sometimes grasp, to the extent that they recognize and exalt Christ as "Son of God," one likewise discovers in the miracles the goodness, sincerity and simplicity which are the most visible qualities of the "Son of man."

In the very way he performs the miracles one notes Jesus' great simplicity, and one might say humility, tact and delicacy of gesture. This is brought home to us by the words which accompanied the raising of the daughter of Jairus: "The child is not dead but asleep" (cf. Mk 5:39), as if he wished to cloak the significance of what he was about to do. And then "he gave strict orders that no one should know this" (cf. Mk 5:43). He did the same in other cases: for example, after curing the deaf mute (cf. Mk 7:36), and after Peter's profession of faith (cf. Mk 8:29-30).

In healing the deaf mute it is significant that Jesus took the man off by himself "away from the crowd." There, "looking up to heaven, he groaned." This "groan" seems to be a sign of compassion and, at the same time, a prayer. The word "Ephphatha!" (Be opened!) has the effect of "opening the ears" and removing "the speech impediment" of the deaf mute (cf. Mk 7:33-35).

If Jesus performs some of his miracles on the sabbath, he does so not to violate the sacred character of the day dedicated to God, but to demonstrate that this holy day is marked in a particular way by God's salvific work. "My Father is at work until now, so I am at work" (cf. Jn 5:17). This work is for the good of humanity, therefore it is not contrary to the holiness of the sabbath, but underlines it: "The sabbath was made for man, and not man for the sabbath! Therefore the Son of man is lord even of the sabbath" (cf. Mk 2:27-28).

If we accept the gospel account of Jesus' miracles—and there is no reason not to accept it other than prejudice against the supernatural—one cannot doubt a unique logic which links together all those "signs" and demonstrates their derivation from God's salvific economy. They serve to reveal his love for us—that merciful love which overcomes evil with good—as is shown by the very presence and action of Jesus Christ in the world. Inasmuch as they are inserted into this economy, the "wonders and signs" are an object of our faith in the plan of God's salvation and in the mystery of redemption effected by Christ.

As facts, the miracles belong to evangelic history, and the accounts contained in the Gospels are as reliable as, and even more so than, those contained in other historical works. It is clear that the real obstacle to the acceptance of Christ's miracles as facts of history and of faith is the anti-supernatural prejudice already referred to. It is a prejudice of those who would limit God's power or restrict it to the natural order of things, as though God were to subject himself to his own laws. But this concept clashes with the most elementary philosophical and theological idea of God—infinite, subsisting and omnipotent Being—who has no limits except in regard to non-existence and therefore the absurd.

One spontaneously notes that this infinity in being and power is also infinity in love, as is demonstrated by the miracles inserted into the economy of the Incarnation and Redemption, as "signs" of the merciful love with which God sent his Son into the world "for us men and for our salvation," generous with us even unto death. *Sic dilexit!* (cf. Jn 3:16)

To such great love let there not be lacking the generous response of our gratitude, expressed in the consistent witness of our lives.

Miracles:
A Call to Faith

The "wonders and signs" which Jesus performed to confirm his messianic mission and the coming of the kingdom of God, are directed and closely linked to the call of faith. This call in relation to the miracle has two forms. Faith precedes the miracle, indeed it is a condition for its accomplishment; faith is an effect of the miracle because it engenders faith in the souls of those who are its recipients or witnesses.

It is known that faith is a human response to the word of divine revelation. The miracle is organically linked with this word of God the revealer. It is a "sign" of his presence and action—a particularly striking sign. All this is a sufficient explanation of the particular link which exists between Christ's "miracles-signs" and faith—a link so clearly outlined in the Gospels.

There is, in fact, in the Gospels a long series of texts in which the call to faith appears as an indispensable and systematic factor of Christ's miracles.

To head the list one must mention the passages concerning the Mother of Christ: how she acted at Cana of Galilee, how she acted earlier, and especially at the moment of the Annunciation. It could be said that precisely here is found the culminating point of her adherence to the faith, which will find its confirmation in Elizabeth's words during the Visitation: "Blessed are you who believed that what was spoken to you by the Lord would be fulfilled" (cf. Lk 1:45). Yes, Mary believed as none other, being convinced that "nothing is impossible for God" (cf. Lk 1:37).

At Cana of Galilee her faith anticipated, in a certain sense, the hour of Christ's self-revelation. Through her intercession he performed that "first miracle-sign," thanks to which Jesus' disciples "believed in him" (cf. Jn 2:11). If the Second Vatican Council teaches that Mary constantly precedes the People of God on the pathways of the faith (cf. *Lumen Gentium,* nn. 58, 63; Encyclical *Redemptoris Mater,* nn. 5-6), we can say that the first foundation of this assertion is already found in the Gospel which gives an account of the "miracles-signs" in Mary and through Mary in regard to the call to faith.

This call is repeated many times. When Jairus, one of the officials of the synagogue, came to ask for his daughter's restoration to life, Jesus said to him, "Do not be afraid: just have faith." (He says "do not be afraid" because some had advised Jairus not to bother Jesus.) (cf. Mk 5:36)

When the father of the epileptic asks for his son's cure, he says: "but if you can do anything...help us." Jesus replies: "If you can! Everything is possible to one who has faith." Then comes the fine act of faith in Christ by this sorely tried man: "I do believe, help my unbelief!" (cf. Mk 9:22-24)

Finally we recall the well-known conversation of Jesus with Mary before the raising of Lazarus: "I am the resurrection and the life.... Do you believe this?... Yes, Lord, I believe..." (cf. Jn 11:25-27).

The same link between the "miracle-sign" and faith is confirmed in the opposite sense by other facts of a negative kind. Let us recall some of them. In Mark's Gospel we read that Jesus of Nazareth "could not perform any mighty deed there, apart from curing a few sick people by laying his hands on them. He was amazed by their lack of faith" (cf. Mk 6:5-6).

We know the gentle rebuke that Jesus once addressed to Peter: "Man of little faith, why did you doubt?" This occurred when Peter began by setting out courageously on the waves to go to Jesus, but then, because of the strong wind, became afraid and began to sink (cf. Mt 14:29-31).

More than once Jesus emphasized that the miracle he worked is linked to faith. "Your faith has saved you," he says to the woman who had been suffering from hemorrhages for twelve years and who came up behind him, touched the hem of his garment and was healed (cf. Mt 9:20-22; Lk 8:48; Mk 5:34).

Jesus spoke similar words when he healed the blind Bartimaeus who was seated by the roadside leading from Jericho. On hearing that Jesus was passing by, Bartimaeus cried out insistently: "Jesus, Son of David, have pity on me" (cf. Mk 10:46-52). According to Mark, Jesus replies: "Go your own way; your faith has saved you." Luke is more precise: "Have sight; your faith has saved you" (cf. Lk 18:42).

Jesus makes a similar statement to the Samaritan cured of leprosy (cf. Lk 17:19).

Two other blind men besought him for the restoration of their sight. Jesus asks them: "Do you believe that I can do this?" "Yes, Lord," they said. Then Jesus said to them: "Let it be done to you according to your faith" (cf. Mt 9:28-29).

Particularly touching is the case of the Canaanite woman who kept on asking Jesus to help her daughter who was "cruelly tormented by a demon." When she prostrated herself before Jesus to beg his assistance, he replied: "It is not right to take the food of the children and throw it to the dogs." (This was a reference to the ethnic diversity between the Israelites and the Canaanites, which Jesus, Son of David, could not ignore in his ordinary behavior. But, he referred to it from a methodological viewpoint to arouse faith.) And then the woman intuitively makes an unusual act of faith and humility. She says: "Please Lord, even the dogs eat the scraps that fall from the table of their masters." Because of these words, so humble, courteous and trusting, Jesus replies: "Woman, great is your faith! Let it be done for you as you wish" (cf. Mt 15:21-28).

It is an event difficult to forget, especially if one thinks of the numerous "Canaanites" of every time, country, color and social condition, who stretch out their hands to ask for understanding and help in their needs!

We should note that the gospel narrative continually stresses the fact that when Jesus "sees their faith," he works the miracle. This is clearly stated in the case of the paralytic who was lowered through an opening in the roof (cf. Mk 2:5; Mt 9:2; Lk 5:20). The same, however, may be said in so many other cases recounted by the evangelists. The element of faith is indispensable, but once that is verified, Jesus' heart is prompt to hear the requests of those in need who turn to him for assistance through his divine power.

Once again we observe, as we stated earlier, that the miracle is a "sign" of God's power and love which save all men and women in Christ. For this very reason, however, it is at the same time a call to faith. It should lead to belief both the one for whom the miracle is worked and the witnesses of the miracle.

This holds true for the apostles themselves, from the very first "sign" Jesus performed at Cana of Galilee; it was then that they "believed in him" (cf. Jn 2:11). Later when he miraculously multiplied the loaves in the vicinity of Capernaum an event linked with the preannouncement of the Eucharist, the Evangelist notes that "from that moment many of his disciples returned to their former way of life and no longer accompanied him." They were unable to accept what appeared to them to be "a hard saying." Jesus then asked the Twelve: "Do you also want to leave?" Peter answers: "Master, to whom shall we go? You have the words of eternal life. We have come to believe and are convinced that you are the Holy One of God" (cf. Jn 6:66-69). The principle of faith therefore is fundamental in the relationship to Christ, both as a condition for obtaining the miracle and as the purpose for which it is performed. This is set out clearly at the end of John's Gospel, where we read: "Jesus did many other signs in the presence of his disciples that are not written in this book. But these are written that you may believe that Jesus is the Messiah, the Son of God, and that through this belief you may have life in his name" (cf. Jn 20:30-31).

Christ's Miracles: Manifestations of the Supernatural Order

Speaking of the miracles which Jesus performed during his earthly ministry, St. Augustine, in an interesting text, interprets them as signs of God's saving power and love and as incentives to raise our minds to the kingdom of heavenly things.

"The miracles worked by our Lord Jesus Christ," St. Augustine writes, "are divine works which raise the human mind above visible things to understand what is divine" (Io. Ev. Tr., 24, 1).

Connected with this thought is the reaffirmation of the close link of Jesus' "miracles-signs" with the call to faith. In fact, these miracles demonstrate the existence of the supernatural order, which is the object of faith. Those who witnessed them, and particularly those who experienced them were made aware, as if by the touch of a hand, that the natural order does not exhaust the whole of reality. The universe in which we live is not limited merely to the range of things accessible to the senses and even to the intellect itself conditioned by sense knowledge. The miracle is a "sign" that this order is surpassed by the "power from on high" and is therefore also subject to it. This "power from on high" (cf. Lk 24:49), namely, God himself, is above the entire natural order and directs this order. At the same time, it [the "power from on high"]—through this natural order and superior to it—makes known that human destiny is the kingdom of God. Christ's miracles are "signs" of this kingdom.

Miracles, however, are not opposed to the forces and laws of nature, but they merely imply a certain empirical "suspension" of their ordinary function—not their annulment. Indeed, the miracles described in the Gospel indicate the existence of a Power superior to the forces and laws of nature, but which at the same time operates according to the demands of nature itself, even though surpassing its actual normal capacity. Is not this what happens, for example, in every miraculous cure? The potentiality of the forces of nature is actuated by divine intervention which extends this potential beyond the sphere of its normal capacity of action. This does not annul or frustrate the causality which God has communicated to created things, nor does it violate the "natural laws" established by God himself and inscribed in the structure of creation. Rather, it exalts and in a certain way ennobles the capacity to operate or even receive the effects of the operation of another, as happens precisely in the cures described by the Gospel.

The truth about creation is the first and fundamental truth of our faith. It is not, however, the only one or the supreme one. Faith teaches us that the work of creation is contained within the ambit of God's plan which, according to his intention, goes well beyond the limits of creation itself. Creation—particularly the human creature called into existence in the visible world—is open to an eternal destiny which is fully revealed in Jesus Christ. Even in Christ the work of creation is completed by the work of salvation. Salvation means a new creation (cf. 2 Cor 5:17; Gal 6:15), a creation according to the measure of the Creator's original design, a re-establishment of what God has made and which in human history had suffered disorder and "corruption" following upon sin.

Christ's miracles enter into the project of the "new creation" and are therefore linked to the order of salvation. They are the salvific "signs" which are a call to conversion and to faith, and in this way, to the renewal of the world subject to "corruption" (cf. Rom 8:19-21).

Therefore, Christ's miracles do not stop at the ontological order of creation *(creatio)* which indeed they touch and set right, but they enter into the soteriological order of the new creation *(re-creatio totius universi)* of which they are the factors, and to which they bear witness as "signs."

The soteriological order is rooted in the Incarnation: the "miracle-signs" of which the Gospels speak also have their foundation in the same reality of the God-Man. This Reality-Mystery embraces and surpasses all the miraculous happenings connected with Christ's messianic mission. It may be said that the Incarnation is the "miracle of miracles," the radical and permanent "miracle" of the new order of creation. God's entrance into the dimension of creation is effected in the reality of the Incarnation in a unique way. To the eyes of faith it becomes a "sign" incomparably superior to all the other miraculous "signs" of the divine presence and action in the world. Indeed, all these other "signs" are rooted in the reality of the Incarnation; they radiate its power of attraction and bear witness to it. They repeat to believers what is written by the Evangelist John at the end of the Prologue on the Incarnation: "We saw his glory, the glory as of the Father's only son, full of grace and truth" (cf. Jn 1:14).

If the Incarnation is the fundamental sign to which are linked all the "signs" bearing witness to the disciples and to humanity that "the kingdom of God has come" (cf. Lk 11:20), there is still an ultimate and definitive sign to which Jesus alludes when quoting the prophet Jonah: "Just as Jonah was in the belly of the whale three days and three nights, so will the Son of man be in the heart of the earth three days and three nights" (cf. Mt 12:40); it is the "sign" of the resurrection.

Jesus prepares the apostles for this definitive "sign" but he does so gradually and tactfully, recommending them to be discreet "until a certain time." There is a particularly clear reference after the transfiguration on the mountain: "As they were coming down from the mountain, he charged them not to relate what they had seen to anyone, except when the Son of man had risen from the dead" (cf. Mk 9:9). One may ask the reason for this. The reply may be that Jesus well knew how complicated the situation might become if the apostles and the other disciples had begun to discuss the resurrection. They were not yet sufficiently prepared to understand it, as appears from the comment of the Evangelist himself in regard to the recommendation just quoted: "They kept the matter to themselves, questioning what rising from the dead meant" (cf. Mk 9:10). Besides, it can be said that the resurrection from the dead, although enunciated and announced, was at the summit of that kind of "messianic secret" which Jesus wished to maintain throughout the entire course of his life and mission until the moment of the final fulfillment and revelation which were verified precisely with the "miracle of miracles"—the resurrection—which, according to St. Paul, is the foundation of our faith (cf. 1 Cor 15:12-19).

After the resurrection, ascension and pentecost, the "miracles-signs" performed by Christ are "continued" by the apostles and later by the saints from generation to generation. The Acts of the Apostles offer us numerous testimonies concerning miracles worked "in the name of Jesus Christ" by Peter (cf. Acts 3:1-8; 5:15; 9:32-41), Stephen (cf. Acts 6:8), and Paul (e.g., cf. Acts 14:8-10). The lives of the saints, the history of the Church, and in particular, the processes for the canonization of the Servants of God, constitute a documentation which, when submitted to the most searching examination of historical criticism and medical science, confirms the existence of the "power from on high" which operates in the natural order and surpasses it. It is a question of miraculous "signs" wrought from apostolic times until the present day, and their essential purpose is to indicate that the human person is destined and called to the kingdom of God. These "signs" therefore confirm in different ages and in the most varied circumstances the truth of the Gospel and demonstrate the saving power of Christ who does not cease to call people (through the Church) to the path of faith. This saving power of the God-Man is manifested also when the "miracles-signs" are performed through the intercession of individuals, of saints, of devout people—just as the first "sign" at Cana of Galilee was worked through the intercession of the Mother of Christ.

Index

apostles 41-42, 43, 47, 66
  miracles performed by, 24-25, 39, 67-68
Augustine, Saint 9-10, 29, 34-35, 63

Cana, miracle of 40, 56
Church, the 41-42
creation 43, 64-65
cross, the 17, 32

evil 29, 31-32

faith 40, 55-60, 68
  and relationship to Christ, 59-60
  object of, 63

God 49, 50-51, 64-65
  merciful love of, 47, 51
  power of, superior to nature, 51, 63
Gospels 14, 39, 47, 48, 51

Incarnation 65-66

Jesus 13, 17, 39-40, 49, 59
  and the power of evil, 29-35
  divine power of, 40
  identity of, 21-24
  merciful love of, 48, 50
  mission of, 32, 49
  presence of, 41-43

kingdom of God 14, 39, 63-64

Lazarus 22, 33-34
love 47, 49-51

Mary 40, 55-56

miracle(s) 16, 29, 39, 51, 55, 63
  calming of the storm, 41-42
  critical-historical aspect of, 8-9, 14-15
  cure of the epileptic, 31
  driving out of demons, 30-32
  in our own day, 8-9, 25, 67-68
  in the apostolic Church, 24-25
  intellectual bias against, 8-10
  Jesus walks on the water, 42
  linked to faith, 55-60, 65
  motive for, 48
  multiplication of the loaves, 41

paralytic of Capernaum, 29-30
power over nature, 23-24, 64
purpose of, 35, 67-68
sign of God's love, 47, 59
sign of Jesus' presence 41-43
sign of the kingdom of God, 64
sign of the new creation, 65

mission 42-43

Peter 13, 24, 42-43, 57, 59

prejudice, anti-supernatural 8-10, 50, 51

resurrection 17, 67

sabbath 15, 50
saints 67-68
salvation 41, 43, 65
salvation history 25
Satan 32, 47. *See also* sin.
science 8-9
sin 29-30, 32, 33, 35, 65
Son of God 13-14, 21, 39-40. *See also* Jesus.
divine power of, 49
Son of man 40, 48. *See also* Jesus.
goodness of, 49-50
soul 29, 35